in memory of Judi Skalsky and David Law

Design is One

design: Massimo Vignelli
graphic production: Piera Brunetta
print production: The Graphic Image Studio Pty Ltd
pre-press: Mission Productions Limited
printing: Max Production Printing & Book-binding Ltd
© 2004 The Images Publishing Group Pty Ltd

ISBN 1 9207 4452 5
Reference number 538

The Images Publishing Group Pty Ltd
Images House
6 Bastow Place
Mulgrave
Victoria 3170
Australia

telephone (613) 9561 5544
facsimile (613) 9561 4860
e-mail: books@images.com.au
internet: www.imagespublishinggroup.com

The following acronyms have been used,
whenever the object is part of the Museum
Permanent Collection:
MoMA-Museum of Modern Art, New York
MET-Metropolitan Museum of Art, New York
BMA-Brooklyn Museum of Art, New York
DNS-Die Neue Sammlung, Munich
MFAH-Museum of Fine Arts, Houston
MAD-Musée des Arts Décoratifs, Montreal

NOTE: The variation in quality of images within this
publication is due to the fact that some have been
taken from archived material. Their lack of quality
in no way reflects the original work.

Lella and Massimo Vignelli: Design is One

I was born and grew up in Milano, Italy, and I started to be interested in architecture when I was 14. At 16, I had my first part-time job as a draftsman in the office of the Architects Castiglioni. They were among the few to work in the entire field of design and of architecture and were already famous for having created radios, flatware, furniture, exhibitions and, of course, architecture as well.

I was fascinated by the scope of their activity. There I learned the famous Adolf Loos dictum that "an architect should be able to design everything from the spoon to the city". From that day, I wanted to design everything…and I have…no cities yet, but lots of spoons!

The basic concept is that the discipline of design is one, and if you can design one thing, you can design everything. The methodology is the same no matter what is the subject.

Lella was born in Udine, on the North East of Italy, an area famous for the entrepreneurial character of its people. Born in a family of famous architects, father, brother and sister, to be an architect for Lella was a matter of genetic trait. We met very young, and we grew up to share our vision of the world and our vision of design.
Somebody said that I perceive what could be done, Lella what can be done.

We are against specialization. We think that it brings entropy and entropy brings creative death. However, in a world that is becoming increasingly more complex, a certain degree of specialization is needed and can be useful…and we can always consult a specialist if necessary. But a total view is necessary.

Design is one. Subjects change materials change, processes change, but the creative and investigative mind proceeds relentlessly with its own discipline through all necessary steps toward the relative solution of the given problems.
I say relative because there is nothing absolute, everything follows your own interpretation of the reality, your own discipline, your own creative force. Time, exposure, focus and determination are the fuel of creativity.

The key to understanding our work, from day one, is quite simple.
We believe that design should be:

Semantically correct. In other words, search for the real meaning and the correct signs that connote the object you are working with.

Syntactically consistent. Every detail must be consistent to itself and to the whole. No borrowed elements. The language is one and every detail should speak the same language.

Pragmatically understandable.
Otherwise, design is a failure, no matter how beautiful it is. Design is not art, design should express its meaning and that should be universally understandable.

Design should also be:

Visually powerful. Otherwise it has no penetrating value. There is no middle ground. Powerful or nothing. Nothingness is not perceivable; therefore, it is not retainable. Period.

Intellectually elegant. Not elegant as mannerism, but intellectually sublime. The opposite of vulgar, because vulgarity is ignorance.
But, above all:

Timeless. Because we have a responsibility to our clients, ourselves and the society in general to design things that will not become obsolete, because obsolescence, particularly planned obsolescence, is a social crime whose ultimate goal is only profit for the few over the masses. And designers should not be part of this despicable conspiracy.

Our ethics demand the best from us in order to give the best to us in return. Design is an encompassing profession, not a job or a trade, but a profoundly ethical profession that we should embrace or reject. No room for the philistines.
No room for the vulgar minds. Ours is a mission to make this world a better place than we found and if we fail our mission, we do not deserve the honor of calling ourselves "designers".

Design is a marvelous mission.
Go out, spread the word.
It is your turn now.

MV

Acknowledgments

From the beginning our work has been made possible by the precious collaboration of many designers who have assisted us in our projects.
Too many to name, they all contributed with passion and dedication to obtain the best.
Particular thanks to our former associates David Law, Michael Bierut and Rebecca Rose, who for many years have shared with us the creative excitement and the pains of delivery.

'55

'60

In the early fifties, I was working as a part-time freelancer in the offices of some of the best Milanese architects, and I was exposed to the excitement of designing everything, "from the spoon to the city". Those formative years left an indelible mark on my approach to the profession; from then on, I wanted to design everything. For me, to design was a mission to prevent bad design from taking place.

From 1955 to 1960, exposed to materials like glass and silver, I made the treasured discovery of merging the craft experience with industrial design.

From 1957 to 1960 Lella and I were awarded fellowships in the United States; that experience became a turning point in our lives. Our mission became clearer and our dedication more determined to succeed. Better design for a better world.

Venini, Light Fixtures, 1955
This series of light fixtures designed for Venini
combines functional and decorative aspects
and provided me with a valuable experience
in the craft of glass making.
MAD

next page:
On the day of our wedding on a cart pushed by
Paolo Venini: Destination USA!

Venini, Glasses, 1957
These drinking glasses feature new vertical striping and color combinations.
MoMA

Venini/Christofle, Glass and Silver Pitchers, 1957
Created originally for an American company, the design was rejected by corporate market research. It was produced later by Venini and Christofle and sold successfully in Europe for several years.

'60

'65

These were the most important years of our career: we discovered our approach and a language to express it.

Seminal projects like the "Piccolo Teatro" and the "Compact" dishes became benchmarks of our design approach. Reminiscent of a Swiss graphic influence, these designs are more dramatic, somehow constructivist, in the choice of black and red; and sometimes are more Mexican as translated from our California experience, with a colorful palette of pink and orange, green and blue, as in the Triennale posters.

The search for objectivity was more interesting to us than subjectivity and our work became increasingly rigorous and primary, as shown by the "Compact" dishes and the Saratoga seating collection.

Piccolo Teatro, Graphic Program, 1964
We first developed the concept of "information bands" separated by bold rulers for this landmark project in which the graphic structure becomes the basic identifier. The concept quickly became a signature of our design.
MoMA

Piccolo Teatro di Milano Ente Autonomo

Direzione Paolo Grassi · Giorgio Strehler

Milano - Palazzo del Broletto - Via Rovello, 2
Telefoni: 896915 - 803464 - 867206 - 867208 - 873585
Biglietteria 872352 - 877663

Ufficio Abbonamenti e Propaganda
Via Rovello, 6

stagione 1964/65 diciannovesima dalla fondazione
al Piccolo Teatro

da sabato 20 febbraio

lunedì, mercoledì, giovedì, venerdì, alle ore 21,10 precise
sabato alle ore 15,30 e 21,10 precise
domenica e festivi alle ore 15,30 precise
termine spettacoli: pomeriggio: ore 18,10, sera: ore 23,50
martedì (esclusi festivi e prefestivi) riposo

La lanzichenecca

2 tempi (5 quadri) di Vincenzo Di Mattia
novità assoluta

regia di Virginio Puecher

Distribuzione:

Cosimo, appaltatore di imprese militari — Arnoldo Foà
Giuditta — Ilaria Occhini
Nullio — Sandro Merli
Tancredi, capitano di ventura — Umberto Ceriani
Fenone, padre di Giuditta — Attilio Ortolani
Jbaldino, suonatore d'arpa — Alfio Petrini
Toga — Paride Calonghi
Liberico — Bob Marchese
Iguccione, reclutatore — Cesare Polacco
il Vescovo Agostino — Armando Alzelmo
...Albigese, capitano di ventura — Alvaro Piccardi
il Cappellano — Sandro Dori
Ottavio — Silvano Piccardi
nonardo, inventore — Alvaro Piccardi
Giustiniano, capitano di ventura — Paride Calonghi
Fier Luigi, suonatore di liuto — Pietro Buttarelli
Gastone, capitano di ventura — Ivan Cecchini
Mauler, rappresentante tedesco — Bob Marchese
addeo — Giorgio Biavati
il Duca — Guido Gheduzzi
rimo funzionario — Alfonso Cassoli
secondo funzionario — Armando Alzelmo
erzo funzionario — Sandro Dori
rimo soldato — Giancarlo Cajo
secondo soldato — Piergiorgio Menegazzo
rimo straccione — Giancarlo Cajo
secondo straccione — Ruggero Dondi
rimo cittadino — Alfonso Cassoli
secondo cittadino — Guido Gheduzzi
erzo cittadino — Ivan Cecchini

ene di Carlo Tommasi
ostumi di Enrico Job
usiche di Raoul Ceroni
sistente alla regia Klaus Michael Gruber

e scene sono realizzate dal Laboratorio
Scenografia del Piccolo Teatro
tobre scenografico Leonardo Ricchelli
struttore Bruno Colombo

tumi sono realizzati dalla Sartoria
el Piccolo Teatro
plicenici: Angelo Bocenti e Ines Razzonico

Direttore di palcoscenico: Luciano Ferroni
Capo elettricista: Mino Campolmi
Primo macchinista: Fortunato Michieli
Rammentatore: Ildebrando Birbò
Attrezzista: Aldo Dal Santo

zzi:

600 Poltrona di platea / **1100** Poltroncina di platea / **800** Balconata

prenotazioni si ricevono alla biglietteria
el Piccolo Teatro (tel. 872352-877663)
ni giorno dalle ore 10 alle ore 19.
prendita e la prenotazione dei posti
gono aperte con quattro giorni di anticipo.
osti prenotati telefonicamente si ritengono
unciati se non vengono ritirati entro le ore 18
el giorno successivo alla prenotazione.

I prezzi qui esposti includono ingresso e tasse
Posteggio autorizzato per automobili.

Vale il tagliando n. 4 degli abbonamenti.

Servizio di recapito a domicilio
dei biglietti e dei posti in abbonamento
prenotati telefonicamente.

o dunque le milizie con le quali un principio
onde il suo stato, o sono sue, o sono
rcenarie, o alleate, o miste. Le milizie
rcenarie e quelle alleate sono inutili e
ricolose; e se un principio fonda la sicurezza
suo stato sulle milizie mercenarie non sarà
ì saldo né sicuro; perché sono milizie disunite,
biziose, infedeli; gagliarde
gli amici, vili con i nemici;
n hanno timore di Dio, né fede con gli uomini;
into si rimanda la rovina, quanto si rimanda
salto; e in pace sei spogliato da loro,
guerra dai nemici. La cagione
questo è che esse non hanno altro amore né
a cagione di guerreggiare che un poco di

stipendio, il che non è sufficiente a far sì che esse
elenco disposte a morire per te.
Vogliono bene essere tuoi soldati finché non
fai guerra, ma come la guerra viene
non desiderano che fuggire o andarsene.

Niccolò Machiavelli da
"Le milizie mercenarie"

Piccolo Teatro di Milano Ente Autonomo

Direzione: Paolo Grassi · Giorgio Strehler

Ufficio - Palazzo del Broletto - Via Rovello, 2
Telefoni: 896915 - 803464
Biglietteria: 872352 - 877663

Ufficio Abbonamenti e Propaganda
Via Rovello, 6
Telefoni: 873585 - 867206

diciannovesima anno dell'Ente

stagione 1964/65 diciannovesima dalla fondazione
al Teatro Lirico
al Piccolo Teatro

Le baruffe chiozzotte
regia di Giorgio Strehler — di Carlo Goldoni

Sul caso di J. Robert Oppenheimer
interpretato da Giorgio Strehler — di Heinar Kipphardt
e David Carpi, Enrico Job, Gigi Lunari, Virginio Puecher, — prima rappresentazione in Italia
Fulvio Fulvetto

Il Signor di Pourceaugnac
regia di Eduardo De Filippo — di Molière
— nuova traduzione di Ruggero Jacobbi

Il gioco dei potenti
da Enrico VI
regia di Giorgio Strehler — Parti I, II, III
— di William Shakespeare

La lanzichenecca
regia di Virginio Puecher — di Vincenzo Di Mattia
— novità assoluta

Il Mistero
regia di Grazia Costa — della Natività, Passione e Resurrezione di Nostro Signore
— laudi medioevali del Secoli XIII e XIV
— riunite ed elaborate da Ettore D'Amico

L'anima buona di Sezuan
regia di Giorgio Strehler — di Bertolt Brecht

Partecipano agli spettacoli, tra gli altri, i seguenti attori
(per ordine alfabetico):
Ladiana Alberti, Armando Alzelmo, Manuele Andrei,
Bambino Barmicoli, Ugo Bassegio, Narciso Bonati, Paolo Borboni,
Giulia Brogi, Tino Buazzelli, Pietro Buttarelli,
Mario Chiocchio, Glauco Chiocchio,
Donatello Ceccarello, Ivan Cecchini, Umberto Ceriani,
Valentina Cortese, Elio Crovetto,
Renato De Carmine, Luciano Dori, Attilio Duse,
Ottavia Fanfoni,

Gianni Garze, Guido Gheduzzi, Gabriele Giocobbe,
Raffaela Giangrande, Giulia Grassi, Vigilio Gottardi, Carlo Grattini,
Franco Graziosi,
Anna Maserati, Mario Moriani, Gianfranco Mauri,
Corrado Nardi, Domenico Negri,
Mario Occhini, Edoardo Onorato,
Corrado Pani, Mino Pegna,
Tino Scotti, Franco Sportelli,
Ferdinando Tamberlani, Marco Tulli,
Mario Valdemarin, Lino Volonghi,

Scene e costumi di Tullio Costa, Luciano Damiani, Enrico Job,
Mino Maccari, Carlo Tommasi,
Musiche di Fiorenzo Carpi, Raoul Ceroni, Paul Dessau, Gino Negri,
Regista assistente: Fulvio Tolusso,
Maestro del Coro: Roberto Leydi,
Maestro di mime: Marise Flach,
Assistenti alla regia: Klaus Michael Gruber, Alberto Negrin, Paolo Radonich,

Capo del servizi tecnici: Bruno Colombo
Direttori di palcoscenico: Bruno Martini, Giancarlo Fortunato,
Vice direttori di palcoscenico: Luciano Ferroni, Nino Manzo,
Capo elettricista: Guglielmo Campolmi
Primi macchinisti: Fortunato Michieli, Guido Romano,
Rammentatori: Corrado Pegorin, Giuseppe Lele,
Attrezzisti: Aldo Dal Santo,
Sarte di palcoscenico: Wera Musetti, Iva Gachelli,
Seconda carnerotta: Gaetanella Birbò
Realizzatori scenografici: Laboratorio di scenografia
del Piccolo Teatro di Milano
Pittore Scenografo: Leonardo Ricchelli,
Costruttore: Bruno Colombo
Confezione dei costumi: Sartoria del Piccolo Teatro di Milano,
Capisartoria: Angelo Bocenti, Tina Mozzetti, Ines Razzonico,

ABBONAMENTI A 5 SPETTACOLI
al cui può la scegliere nelle alternative proposte

6500 Poltrona di platea / **4200** Poltroncina di platea / **3300** Balconata

Tagliando n. 1 per "Le Baruffe Chiozzotte"
Tagliando n. 2 per la tariffica da scegliere tra:
- il Caso di J. Robert Oppenheimer, o il Signor di Pourceaugnac
Tagliando n. 3 per "Il gioco dei potenti - (da Enrico VI)"
Tagliando n. 4 per la seconda da scegliere tra:
- La Lanzichenecca, o il Mistero
Tagliando n. 5 per "L'Anima buona di Sezuan"

Diritto di prenotazione preventiva gratuita di comunicazioni a biglietteria
del Teatro via la rintracciata di richiesta.
Abbonamenti in gennaio della Piccola Teatro

L'abbonamento da diritto ad esclusivo ad una tariffa questionali
ove alla propria complicabilità con le discontabilità della stata,
non alle spalato tenere, pressante tassina, dante e cassi.

La Direzione del Piccolo Teatro si riserva di spostare o modificare,
per comuni cause di forza maggiore
gli spettacoli in abbonamento e le relative ore e ore in altro sedi.

Per qualsiasi altra informazione e per ogni chiarimento,
l'interessato può rivolgersi all'Ufficio Abbonamenti del Piccolo Teatro,
via Rovello 6 telefoni 873 585 - 867 206

Gli abbonamenti si ricevono alla biglietteria del Piccolo Teatro
Via Rovello 2, telefoni 872 352 - 877 663
dalle ore 10 alle ore 20 a cominciare da sabato 10 ottobre.

I prezzi di abbonamento sono comprensivi di ingresso e tasse

31st and 32nd Biennale d'Arte, Venice, 1962 and 1964

These posters, which define light as the only element shared by all art forms, are part of a graphic program for the Biennale d'Arte of Venice, an international exhibition of the arts.
MoMA

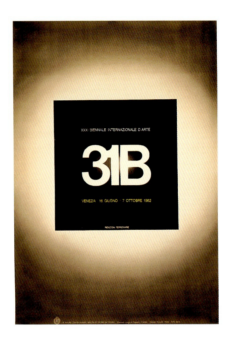

Biblioteca Sansoni, 1963
To establish the format for this series of paperback books, we turned the titles sideways to introduce large-sized type and reach greater impact at point of sale. This approach proved to be economical, effective and less controversial.

Biblioteca Sansoni

Henri Pirenne — Storia d'Europa, dalle invasioni al XVI secolo

G. Volpe — Il Medio Evo

É. Dolléans — Storia del movimento operaio 1 / 1830-1871

Uomo e mito nelle società primitive, a cura di C. Leslie

Compact Stacking Dinnerware, 1964
This ubiquitous melamine dinnerware, designed to be stackable in a compact way, originally was manufactured in Italy and won our first Compasso d'Oro Award for Good Design in 1964. Introduced later in the United States and manufactured by Heller, the dinnerware became extremely popular, especially after it was produced in a rainbow of brilliant colors. This timeless design still is in production.
MoMA

Poltronova, Saratoga Furniture, 1964
This comprehensive line of lacquered furniture and its boxy design, the first of its kind in the marketplace, established a trend for years to come. Designed to have a built-in look, the furniture's glossy hard edges contrast with the soft, matte leather of the pillows.

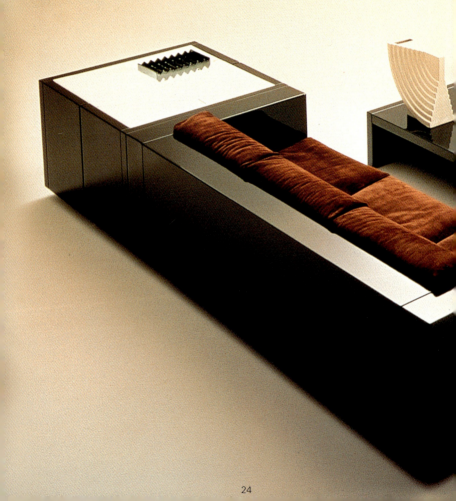

'65

'70

In 1965, with Ralph Eckerstrom, a designer from Chicago, Jay Doblin and other friends, we started Unimark International. The work of this period reflects our intention to bring design to large international corporations. Some of the projects are corporate identities for mega companies like Ford, JC Penney, Knoll International, the Transit Authorities of New York City and Washington, D.C., American Airlines, etc.

I was in charge of design worldwide, and, in a few years, we had offices in Chicago, New York, Detroit, Cleveland, Denver, San Francisco, Milano, London, Copenhagen, Johannesburg and Melbourne. Too many and too much! New York was our office, and there we accomplished many innovative projects.

In old Europe, every trade and profession had
its own color of smock. Typographers and printers
wore black smocks, mechanics blue, upholsterers
khaky, houseware clerks grey and so on.
Doctors and architects wore white smocks.
The white smock connoted immediatly that you
were a professional, not a dilettante, and that is
exactly why I was wearing a white smock.
At a time when our profession was less
established than today, I wanted very much to
stress the notion that designers were professionals
like the architects, not dilettantes playing with
color, form and type.
The white smock, covering our clothing and
personality, was a great equalizer, stressing
objectivity over subjectivity, which, at that time,
was at the core of our philosophy. We were
against the prevarication of the individual over the
collective, of one being over the other for his own
sake. It was part of the big dream, the utopia of
the modern movement, of which I was a
passionate believer, and to an a extent I still am....
When we started Unimark offices around the
world in 1965, we were wearing the white smock
in every office until one day in 1970, the Chicago
office started a revolt: no more white smocks!
All of a sudden, in those hippy years, the white
smock had become the symbol of corporate power,
of the oppressor, and that was the end of it. The
blue jean then took its place.

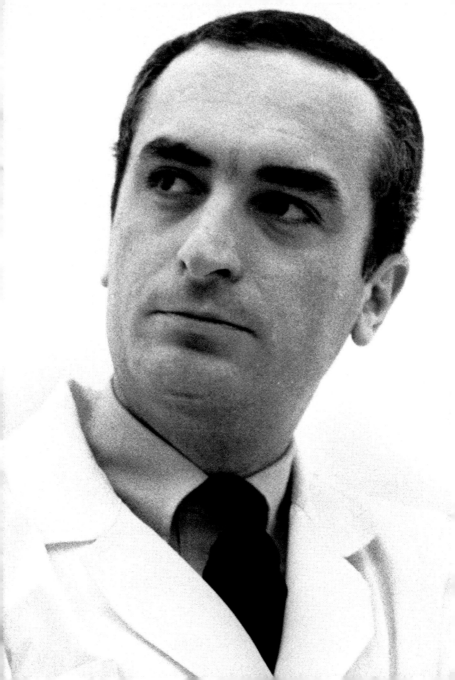

New York Subways

New York Metropolitan Transit Authority, Subway-Sign System, 1966
Contrary to the customary design tradition existing at the time, we devised a modular system of panels that could combine any kind of appropriate message to make any kind of subway sign. The system includes panels of 1'x1' for line identification and direction; 1'x2' for information; 1'x4' for direction; and 1'x8' for station identification. The panels are suspended from a black channel, graphically reinforcing the message. To discourage graffiti, the surface later was changed from white to black, but the information structure remains unchanged.

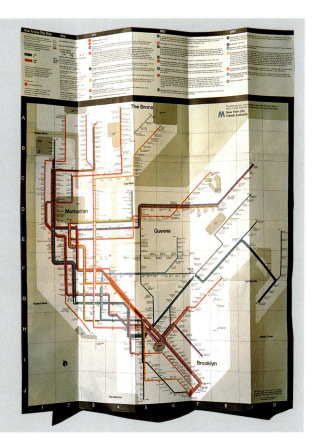

New York MTA, Subway Map, 1970
Following up on the subway-sign system, we were asked to design a new subway map. Based on a 45- and 90-degree grid, we created a clear and simple map without fragmentation where every subway line was identified with a color and every station with a dot. No dot, no station, period. The geography, based on the same grid, follows the level of abstraction of the subway-lines map as an integral part of the message. This map, unfortunately, was replaced with a disorderly and fragmented design by new management. These things happen....
MoMA

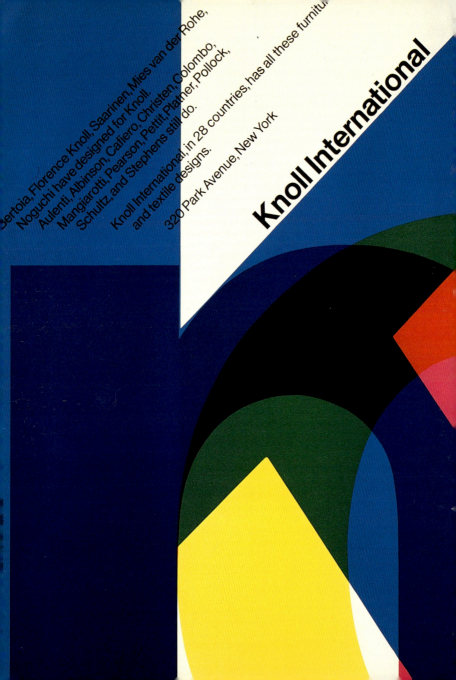

Bertoia, Florence Knoll, Saarinen, Mies van der Rohe, Noguchi have designed for Knoll. Aulenti, Albinson, Catiero, Christen, Colombo, Mangiarotti, Pearson, Pettit, Platner, Pollock, Schultz, and Stephens still do.
Knoll International, in 28 countries, has all these furniture and textile designs.
320 Park Avenue, New York

Knoll International

previous pages:
Knoll International, Poster, 1966
Knoll is so well known for its contemporary classic furniture that we felt we could play with its name. On the backside of the poster, line drawings illustrate the entire furniture collection.
MoMA

Knoll International, Graphic Program, 1966–1980
For many years we designed all printed matter for Knoll, an outstanding furniture company and world leader in its field. The catalogs, price lists and brochures became benchmarks for furniture companies around the world. Knoll's design commitment made our collaboration an exciting and productive experience.
A great client brings more great clients; conversely, a bad one brings worse ones.

American Airlines, Corporate Identity, 1967
We were introduced to this assignment by Henry Dreyfuss, the legendary designer who was a consultant to American Airlines. The one-word AmericanAirlines logo…half-red, half-blue, in plain type…stresses the professional, no-gimmicks attitude of the company in the colors of its home nation. Still in use today, this logo is one of the few worldwide that needs no change.

Heller, Packaging Program, 1968
Aiming to identify and connect Heller with a new line of design-conscious products, we decided to keep the name the same size on all the boxes, regardless of size, and cropping when necessary. The orange type on the white box at the point of sale became a banner for what the company represents: "good design at affordable prices".

Dot Zero Magazine, 1966/1969
As one of the intellectual extravagances of Unimark International, a company that we cofounded in 1965 in Chicago, we published a magazine addressing monographic issues and design topics. It was a terrific magazine with great contributors, from Marshal Mc Luhan to Herbert Bayer, from Jay Doblin to Mildred Constantine. It was fun to design it and provided us with the opportunity to do typographic experimentation, and do things that no other magazine could do at that time.

"Industrial Design", 1967–1970

"Industrial Design" was the first magazine that we designed in the United States. Because the design was based on a grid format, we could accommodate all situations and, importantly, could design the magazine in a single day, achieving the desired tension and speeding the production process. Magazine design based on a grid was unusual at that time, so this became an opportunity to explore new ground.

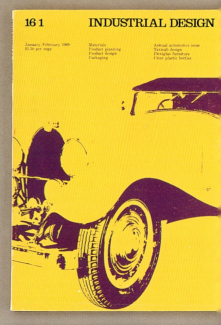

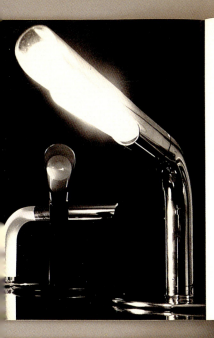

Design in action

Some elegant lighting fixtures from Germany and the first transistor operated clock made in Italy are included in this month's portfolio of designs.

Part of the OMK "T" range are these knock-down, stacking chairs. Frames are either polished chrome or nylon coated for outdoor use with waterproof canvas or leather slung seats.

The "Chronotime" is a desk or wall clock made in three sections—the first two form the clock body and the third the clock holding ring. Different body shapes may be obtained by rotating the two body sections in opposite directions. The dial can be adjusted by turning the clock holding ring. The Chronotime is the first transistor-operated clock made in Italy. It is powered by a battery with a life of nearly 18 months. The body is injection casted and assembled by pressure injection using ABS. Pio Manzu is the designer.

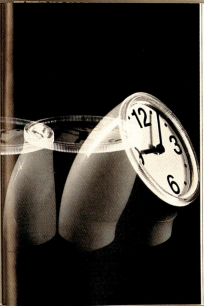

'70

'75

In the 1970s, we left Unimark and opened our own office, Vignelli Associates, in New York. Our client list included Knoll, Bloomingdale's, Minneapolis Museum of Fine Arts and other clients of all sizes. However, we were very selective, knowing that a bad client brings a worse one next time.

We preferred projects where we could do our best, without compromise or fear, dealing most of the time with enlightened clients in charge of their own businesses. No middle management terrorized of making mistakes! No focus groups on our landscape!

Here we are, working together, in our new
Vignelli Associates office in New York.
By that time Lella could dedicate herself
full time to the office and we could take larger
interiors projects. One of the first was to design
the interiors and architectural graphics for
the Minneapolis Museum of Fine Arts,
whose plans lay on the table before us.
Many more will follow in the years to come.

the HERALD

35c

CIA in Cambodia: the real story
Answers to year-old questions, page 3

Harry Van Arsdale: Ebbing of power
Cabbies show away from founding father, page 2.

Drugs: legal and illegal
The ethical drug industry faces new regulations, section 2, page 7

Larry Rivers designs a dress
And THE HERALD designs a world to fit, section 2, page 11

The peace movement: a week before Washington
THE HERALD reports on the movement as it is today, page 7

Creativity and making music
Patti Smith tells what goes on inside a recording studio, page 9

April 18, 1971

No one argues that Bella Abzug isn't an event in Washington. THE HERALD spent time talking and walking with, and listening to, the freshman Congresswoman from Manhattan's West Side.

Bella Abzug: power to Congress
The hard campaigner as a tough Representative

by Louis Sepersky

[article text]

Diamonds in Vietnam
New facets of the sinewing PX scandal

by Clark Mollenhoff

Spying on Congress
"It is a threat to our freedom. Surveillance leads to fear."

Changing faces in Moscow
The 24th Communist Party Congress changes staff and softens peace

46

BRUSSELS	U.K.	EUROPE/U.S.	GERMANY	FRANCE	EEC
Is NATO obsolete?	Sterling pound gains against dollar	Euroconsumism does not exist: Longo/Kissinger	Is the Baader terror linked to the Italian one?	A mysterious wave of antisemitism	Elections when?

New terror in Rome. Postal employee shot in the legs

Otto Grunder, 43, a career diplomat is Bonn's spy from East

North Sea oil spill won't endanger quality of water

THE EUROPEAN JOURNAL

The only European daily in America   La Stampa / Die Welt / Le Monde / The Times with The Observer

The jobless in Germany will be more than 2 million

Mitterand tells of his meeting with Carter: They never spoke about PCF

How Callaghan has won the fight with the firefighter

47

previous pages:
"The Herald", 1971
In 1971, there were few well-designed newspapers in the world. "The Herald" project allowed us to open up the field and design a newspaper on a grid of six columns and 16 modules high with one typeface: one size for text, two sizes for titles and italic for captions; one module for titles. There were few exceptions. The grid provides flexibility to the layouts and sped up the design and production processes.

"The European Journal", 1978
A few years after designing "The Herald", we were asked to design another daily newspaper: "The European Journal". As before, we structured the paper on a modular grid to optimize design and production time. Unfortunately, the project was not realized.

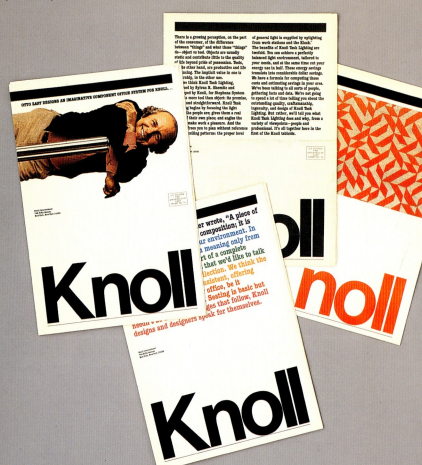

Knoll, 1972
After designing sleek brochures for Knoll over time, we decided to experiment with the tabloid format. Printed in four colors on newsprint paper, the Knoll tabloid was a complete novelty at the time and an exciting experience that allowed us to explore new territory.

"Knoll au Louvre, Paris", 1971
For the "Knoll au Louvre" exhibit, we restored a 45-foot-high wing of the museum and designed 8-foot-high cubes in which the furniture was presented in proper scale. We placed audiovisual cubes on top of some of the furniture cubes to master the height of the space. The cubes, on casters, could be moved and placed in different locations and alignments.

Knoll International, Catalog, 1971
We designed the catalog with photographs by Herbert Matter for the memorable "Knoll au Louvre" exhibition.

Bloomingdale's, Graphic Program, 1972
After we opened our new office in New York City, one of our first projects was the graphic program for Bloomingdale's, at that time the essence of New York...a department store on the high-end side. We designed the packaging, signage and a logo in three weights to be used for the appropriate merchandise, boxes in eight different bright colors, and an exclusive alphabet for advertising and signage. It is a bright and articulated program that reflects the liveliness of the store. The shopping bags are, by now, a New York landmark.

bloomingdale's
bloomingdale's
bloomingdale's

Massimo and Lella in a kind of hippy mood of the time…

Heller, Stacking Cups, 1970
In Europe, coffee cups are filled halfway, but
In the United States, they are filled to the top.
Here is the problem: the coffee finds the opening
at the top of the cup and drips down the handle,
down to the saucer and onto the table.
What a shame! It could have been enough to
merely pour less coffee, but everyone asked us to
close the opening, so the design was modified:
I was furious!
MoMA

Heller Stacking Mugs, 1972; Pitcher, 1978
The mug is the direct descendent of the cups
without the opening at the top of the handle.
No complaints this time, on the contrary, a
tremendous success made the mugs ubiquitious
and widely copied by other manufacturers....
In 1978, we added the pitcher. When the lid is
aligned with the handle, it means the spout is
open; otherwise, the spout is closed.
A simple case of applied semiotics.

Heller, Glass Bakeware, 1970
Designed to go from the oven to the table, the Heller bakeware incorporates a handle all around the perimeter, a lid that doubles as a casserole, and engraved glass to add sparkle and eliminate transparency. Remember, food is prettier in plan view than in section.
MoMA

Minneapolis Museum of Fine Arts, 1974
Our approach to the design of the interiors and display cases for the Minneapolis museum, restructured by architect Kenzo Tange, was to understate the presence of structures supporting the works of art and to design display cases that were almost invisible. We wanted our design not to interfere with the art, but to interact with the architecture of the old and new wings of the museum.

Stendig Calendar, 1966
The Stendig calendar is, by now, an American institution, published every year since 1966! Its large size, 100x140 cm, makes it visible across any large room and its design has generated countless imitations. By one incredible circumstance, it went directly from the printer to the Museum of Modern Art, New York's permanent collection.

Wild Places Calendar, 1975
The Wild Places calendar unfolds like a book and doubles its size.

Nava Calendar, 1976
The Nava calendar is a perpetual calendar, but you have to turn a page every day. It measures 30x30 cm.

Minneapolis Museum of Fine Arts, 1974
Old wing gallery.

1986 February

M	T	W	T	F	S	S
					1	2
3	4	5	6	7	8	9
10	11	12	13	14	15	16
17	18	19	20	21	22	23
24	25	26	27	28		

23

August '75

Sunday	Monday	Tuesday	Wednesday	Thursday	Friday	Saturday
					1	2
3	4	5	6	7	8	9
10	11	12	13	14	15	16
17	18	19	20	21	22	23
24/31	25	26	27	28	29	30

’75

In these years, we worked with a fantastic array of great clients with thrilling projects. Saint Peter's Church in Manhattan, where we designed everything from the space to the accessories; Joseph Magnin in California, where we created a series of stores with a highly flexible and unique system of display; and corporate identities for Lancia cars and Ciga hotels, a super-deluxe chain of grand hotels throughout Italy. For Ciga, we designed everything…graphics, silverware, glassware, etc. A landmark project.

Those were the years of the publications for the Institute of Architecture and Urban Studies, and above all, the publications system for the United States' National Park Service, a project brought to us by Vincent Gleason, then director of publications for NPS.
A memorable project that resulted in the USA Presidential Design Award.

Saint Peter's Church, New York, 1977
Interior

Saint Peter's Church, New York, 1977

The interior design program for Saint Peter's Church required a high degree of flexibility. Beyond its normal liturgical functions, the church acts as a concert hall, theater and conference hall. A series of steps beside the movable pews were designed to convert into additional seats. Several platforms can be adjusted to suit different needs for different events.
We designed the organ and placed it on a corner to amplify the acoustics. On the opposite side, granite steps descend into a baptismal font. We also designed the furniture, the altar, the silver accessories for the functions and the graphics for the church, including the symbol and the publications.
Saint Peter's Church was a unique experience, a total design concept for a place that is conceived not simply as a church, but as a moral space for a variety of functions.
DNS

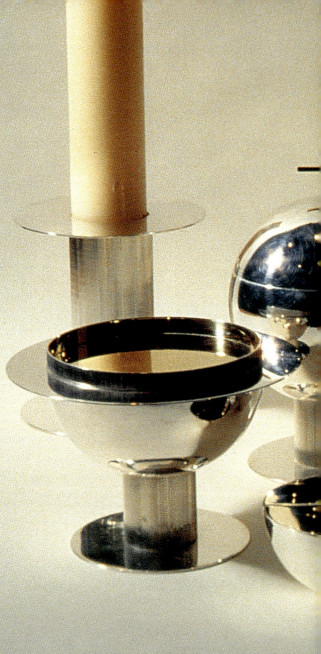

BMW Traveling Auto Show, 1976
For the BMW traveling auto show, we created a series of light boxes with graphics that could be arranged in several ways to adapt to different space conditions, and provide dramatic illumination of the cars. The opposite side of the light boxes was covered in reflective stainless steel; the floor was Pirelli rubber. The message: "the ultimate driving machine".

following page:
Joseph Magnin stores, California, 1978
Conceived not as a retail temple, but as a dynamic bazaar, we designed the Joseph Magnin stores as a system of highly flexible components, movable on casters, but permanent in appearance. The system includes peripheral booths, movable rack and display cases, fitting rooms, cash register stations and seating...all designed to interact among themselves and with the merchandise. And, if one arrangement does not work, it can be turned around in a few minutes to organize a better one. In the following pages, we see the system's components and a retail shoe area.

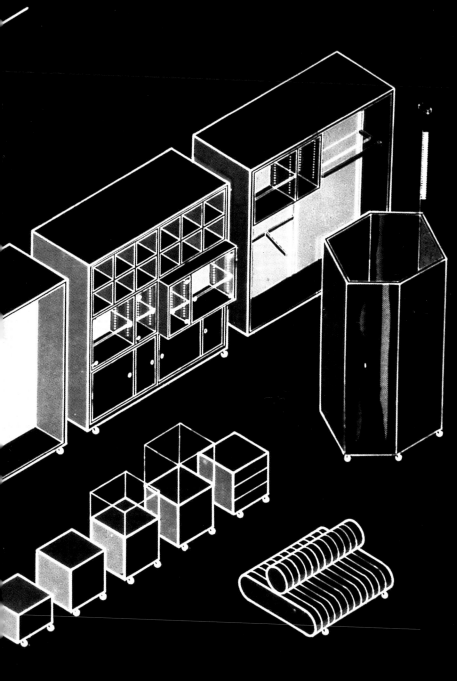

Institute for Architecture and Urban Studies, New York, Graphic Program, 1976
This comprehensive and seminal program, ranging from posters to books, magazines to tabloids, had a tremendous impact in the architectural publications world.

next page:
Bicentennial Poster, 1976
This poster celebrates not a melting pot, but the lively interaction of the different ethnic groups that make the United States.

United States National Parks Service, Washington, D.C., Publications Program, 1977
In order to achieve better identification and financial savings through standardization of every aspect of the publications program, we designed a modular system that determined everything from the paper size to graphics to cartography and illustration. We devised a black band at the top of the printed pieces identifying the park and a limited range of typefaces for the text. The information is organized in horizontal bands of text and images. The Park Service designers were encouraged to achieve their best within these parameters. The results have been extremely gratifying and this program has been acclaimed the world over for its efficiency, identity and intellectual elegance. In 1985, we were presented the US Presidential Design Award for this work.

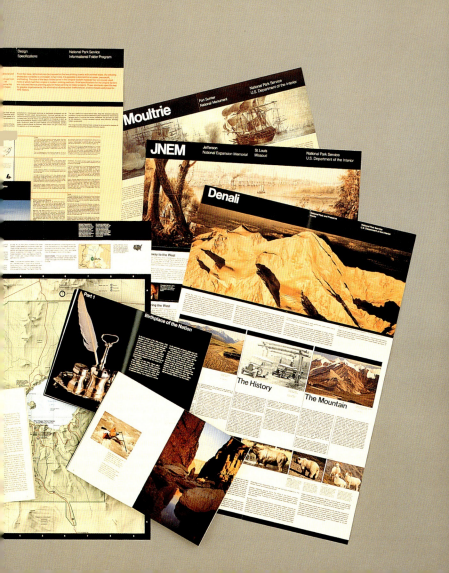

"Faces", Chanticleer Press, New York, 1977
A short, rather than a long title produces a
stronger cover on a book, so we changed the
original title for greater effectiveness.
In this book, about the history of portrait
photography, no picture could be cropped.
It was a good exercise of layout discipline.

**Audobon Society Field Guides, Knopf,
New York, 1976–78**
The Audobon Society guides were designed
with a waterproof cover and pocket sized to take
out in the field. To our great satisfaction, they have
been a bestseller for many years and set the
style for other guides thereafter.

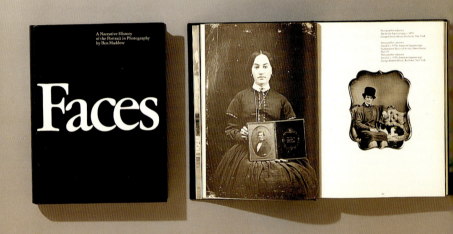

Lancia, Corporate Identity Program, 1978
This comprehensive project for Lancia included all printed matter, advertising formats, service and dealer signage. First, we had to revive and redesign the old logo that had been abandoned in favor of a meaningless one. Logos, when old, are part of our visual culture and should be protected. This program received considerable praise from Lancia's customers.

CIGA Hotels, Italy, 1979

In a situation similar to Lancia, CIGA had a long history and its trademark was well known. Therefore, we preserved and redesigned it for more effective use. We chose glossy black as a formal and festive chromotype and the elegant Bodoni typeface for all printed matter. The super ellipse of the logo became the matrix for many of the objects we designed for CIGA.

CIGA, Glasses and Pitcher, 1979
The corrugation of the glass surface, inspired by the domes of Venetian churches, creates shadows and reflections, which add brilliance and elegance and bring life to a common material. MET

CIGA, Silverware, 1979
As part of the overall design program for CIGA, we designed all the hotel silverware and hollow-ware, based on the motif generated by the flatware in this picture.
DNS

Casigliani, Italy, Kyoto Dinnerware, 1979
This set of Kyoto dishes was designed to make a "clean pile of dirty dishes" at the end of a meal. All leftovers and flatware slide into the deep dish, one plate on top of the other, covered by a small dish at the top of the pile, and left on the table.

Casigliani, Italy, Metafora 1 Coffee Table, 1979
We like to design furniture in which the user can participate in the final configuration. Each piece, then, becomes quite different, but without a loss of identity. The Metafora 1 table demonstrates this concept, since you can position the four marble pieces any way you like them, but the object remains the same. Many of the tables we have created for Casigliani reiterate this concept.

SunarHauserman, Rotonda Chair, 1979
The shape of the Rotonda chair, inspired by a Mexican chair, is derived from the natural stretch of the fabric between the top and bottom frames. The chair has a tubular frame and molded-foam cushion covered in fabric.

'80

'85

The work done in previous years begins to produce cherished rewards from our peers. Our design language is ripening and some of the best projects of our career came out of these years.

The Italcenter and Hauserman showrooms reflect our predilection for primary shapes and minimal environments. Our design becomes stronger and wittier in the use of color, as in the Miami showroom for Artemide.

Our position against the excesses and provincialism of postmodernist design becomes a commitment to keep the values of the modern movement alive.

In the early seventies, the theme of the Aspen Design Conference was "Italian Design", and we were invited to give a speach on our work.
We were scheduled for a night performance in the big tent with an audience of about 2000 people. We asked to have two stools on an empty stage, a big screen for the projection, total darkness and only two lights on the two of us.
What a dramatic set! That night, dressed in black, Lella in a terrific Missoni sweater, for the first time we told the story of our life...It was great!

Kroin, Corporate Identity, 1981–1985
A perfect example of the impact of a chromotype in an identification program. Everything for Kroin, from stationery to literature, from packaging to interiors became immersed in the strong yellow color. Catalog sheets could be folded to become mailers, data sheets, advertising pages. A very substantial program developed with great economy of means and with remarkable impact. It still is fresh and strong twenty years thereafter….

Knoll, Books, 1981
Created in 1981, the "Knoll Design" book is a

Knoll, Handkerchief Chair, 1982–1987
After many years in product development, the
Handkerchief chair was produced finally and,
somehow, heavier than desired. However, it
became a classic for its proportion and elegance.
Designed with David Law, it is one of our
best products.
MoMA, BMA, MFAH

Vignelli Exhibition at Parsons, New York, 1980
The announcement for the Vignelli exhibition was printed using Bodoni type in a classical, rhetorical way on tissue papers of different colors.
The tissue papers then were wrinkled to undeceive the pompousness of the message and achieve an interesting distortion of the type. Some recipients got the message; others complained that the invitation arrived wrinkled.

"Architectural Record", 1982
For several years we designed every issue of "Architectural Record" based on a grid system to assure consistency and continuity of design quality and to achieve speed of production.

next pages:
Italcenter Showroom, Chicago, 1982
For us, to design interiors is to create memorable spaces. For this furniture showroom for ten different Italian manufacturers we designed a series of parallel spaces divided by a central corridor in which a large golden sphere, a pyramid and cylinders imparted a memorable presence to the space.

Hauserman Showroom, Los Angeles, 1982
The Hauserman showroom was about movable walls. With the walls, we created a series of corridors, each with a different light installation by the artist Dan Flavin. It was an incredible experience, a great art installation.

IDCNY, Corporate Identity, 1983 and 1989
This program, designed for the International Design Center, New York, is based on a red chromotype and black-on-white Bodoni typeface. With great economy of means, this program achieved considerable impact and set the standard for similar organizations.

Fratelli Rossetti, Graphic and Packaging Program, 1984
For Fratelli Rossetti, an Italian shoe manufacturer, we created a logo and logo pattern to be used throughout the program for boxes, shoe lining, shopping bags, etc.

IBM, Personal Computer Manuals, 1984
For the introduction of the IBM PC, we designed the packages and software manual, creating, instead of the industry's usual cheap plastic binders, hard-bound linen covers and slipcovers in pastel colors to stress cultural elegance and personal values.

**Artemide Showroom, Dallas, 1984;
Miami, 1985**

The basic notion of these showrooms for the
lighting company, Artemide, was to display each
family of products in a separate space to avoid
visual noise and increase effectiveness and
memorability. The Dallas showroom was made
with particle-board panels resembling limestone.
The Miami showroom, based on the same
concept, uses color in a playful manner
appropriate to that city.

Cleto Munari, Silver Tea Set, 1984
This tea set was commissioned to join others designed by famous architects of that postmodern time when it seemed that the snake of reaction to modernism would destroy the purity and minimalism of Euclidean geometry...and, in doing so, became a perfect postmodern metaphor.

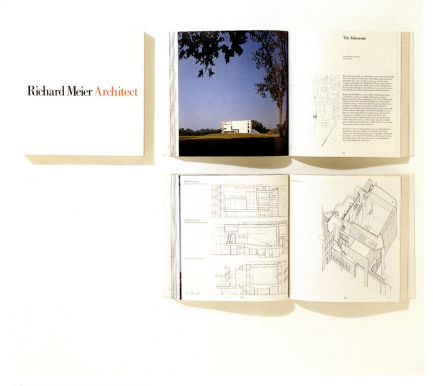

"Richard Meier, Architect", 1984
This is the first of a series of books on the work of the architect Richard Meier that reflects the character of his buildings: structured, subjective and, above all, not trendy.

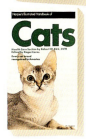

**Cats and Dogs Guides, Harper & Row,
New York, 1985**
Every detail of these books was carefully planned, from charts to the photography on white backgrounds, to achieve maximum clarity and objectiveness. They still are the best guides to pets.

Acerbis, Serenissimo Table, 1985
This table stresses the contrast between the heaviness of the legs and the thinness of the top. The legs are in steel covered with "Venetian stucco", an interesting revival of a traditional technique. The top, in glass, creates the look of thin and thick not dissimilar from that of a Bodoni typeface. Another example that "Design is One".

Casigliani, Pisa Table, 1985
Again, a design stretching "identity and diversity":
the position of the vertical slab or the slanted
column can be changed in any way, but the
identity of the table remains.

Casigliani, Mesa Table, 1985
The troncated cone base is separated from the
top of the table by a cilinder of rusted steel that
provides strength and stability.

'85

'90

In 1985, we relocated our office to
a beautiful new space with great views
of the New York skyline and Hudson
River. Completely designed by us, the
office became a testing ground for
materials, such as particle board for walls
and cubicles, lead for walls and doors,
corrugated metal for walls, and
a special resin-and-sand compound
for the floor. Blue, white and brown steel,
sometimes covered with gold leaf.
An ambiguous play between monastic
and sensual feelings.
Book design, furniture and interior
designs, chinaware, silverware and
glassware designs. These years are
rich with our involvement across the
whole area of design, including sets and
formats for TG2, the Italian second
television channel. Exciting years of
experimentation and the expression of
our language. And, as we look back,
happy years of brilliant and, sometimes,
mind-boggling successes.

Vignelli Associates Office, New York, 1985
In 1985 we moved to a new office space with spectacular views of the Manhattan skyline and the Hudson River. The space was completely designed by us in a most serene way and it offered the opportunity of testing ideas and materials against time. We used raw steel for tables; lead for some walls and doors; particle board for walls, shelves and work stations; aluminum grids brushed randomly to contradict the grid; sandblasted glass; corrugated galvanized steel to separate the office from the service area; Dexotex floors; gold leaf on raw steel tubing as table bases; and ordinary materials in extraordinary ways. In the year 2000 we lost our lease and had to move out. End of an era… on to the next.

Acerbis, Creso Table, 1985
Originally designed for our office, this table combines a raw steel tubular base covered in gold leaf, and a glass top. Chosen by a manufacturer, Acerbis, it became a product.

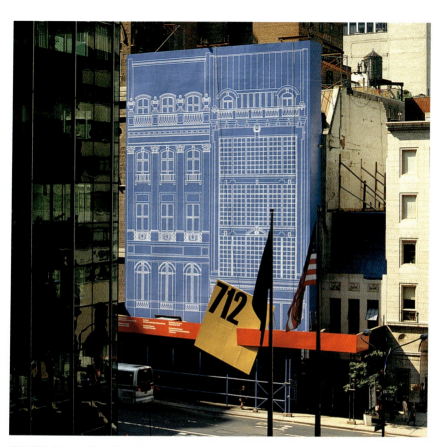

712 Fifth Avenue, New York, Construction Barricade, 1987
To reassure New Yorkers that the two townhouses would be preserved in front of a new skyscraper, we placed a full-sized blueprint on the barricade. The red ribbon piercing through the yellow square contributes information and surprise to the liveliness of the street.

Artemide Showroom at IDCNY, New York, 1987
Placed in a loft-like space, the elements of this showroom interact with the raw space with a deliberate play between finished and unfinished materials in a museum-like installation of objects on pedestals or dedicated spaces.

Poltrona Frau, Stand, Salone del Mobile, Milano, 1988
Instead of displaying Poltrona Frau's furniture, which was shown in another space, we displayed photographs of splendid installations of the company's furniture in landmark palaces mounted on galvanized steel panels on galvanized steel stela resting on a galvanized steel floor. The walls were illuminated from the bottom up, giving a sense of levitation to the entire space. Only one piece of furniture, the company icon, was exhibited on a glass platform on the floor.

Poltrona Frau, Exhibition Space, Tolentino, Italy, 1988
Carved out of the factory building, this showroom space is preceded by an open-air, cubic atrium leading to the space and the auditorium on one side.

Poltrona Frau, Auditorium, Tolentino, Italy, 1988
Adjacent to the exhibition space is the auditorium. Walls and ceiling are covered with perforated metal with acoustic material behind it. All furniture was specifically designed for this space.

Poltrona Frau, CEO Office Furniture Line, 1988
Designed to stand free from the walls, this furniture line, covered in precious leather, has a desk that pivots on a pedestal-cabinet to provide different configurations.

United States Postal Service, 1987
Designed to complement the "factory" building developed by the architectural firm of Jones Mah Gaskill & Rhodes, we had to devise a front that could be identified as the post office with a recognizable identity but, at the same time, be compatible with each regional context.
We designed a modular façade identical as a system, but different as materials, according to the region: brick in Maryland, limestone in Illinois, white metal panels in Maine and stucco in Florida. A gallery behind the façade connects the different areas for the public.

Sasaki, Colorstone Dinnerware, 1985
Decoration is usually obtained by adding something. Since our design process is based on subtraction, we obtained decoration by removing the glaze from the edges, exposing the material. An unusual, but effective way to achieve product identity.
With David Law.

Sasaki, Classico Goblets, 1986
A series of crystal goblets of equal height, but different diameters. A perfectly joined cup, stem and base makes this classic form unusually elegant.

Sasaki, Basic Flatware, 1987
A line of flatware, so basic in its simplicity that it became its name. The elegance of its form and balance makes this usual form unusual.
With David Law.

Palio Hollowware, 1987
Originally designed for the Palio restaurant in Manhattan, this line was obtained by complementing existing parts with new handles, spouts and tops. It became a fast, inexpensive and unique design.

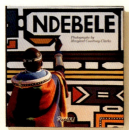

"Ndebele", Rizzoli International, New York, 1986
Beautiful photography by Margaret Courtney Clarke documents the vanishing art of a South African tribe, painted by anonymous women.

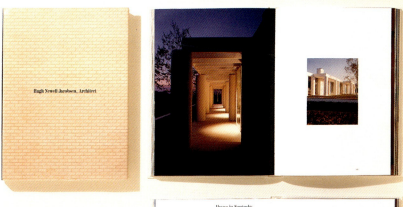

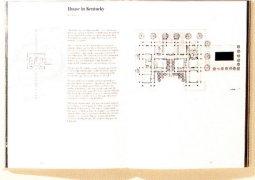

**"Hugh Newell Jacobsen, Architect",
AIA Press, Washington, D.C., 1988**
A book on the passionate work of a remarkable American architect, devoted to the play of beautiful living in an architecture sensitive to its context and territory. A master of intellectual elegance. Two more volumes followed.

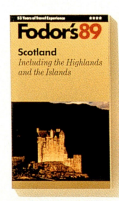

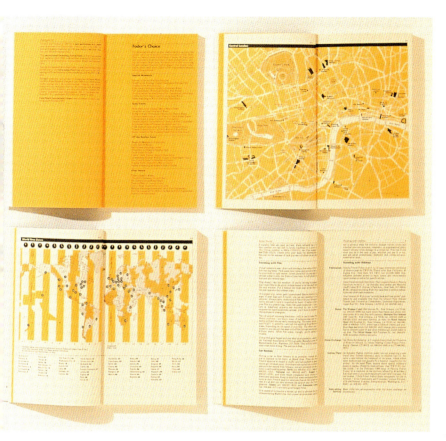

Fodor's Travel Guides, New York, 1988
A complete redesign of these popular guides, read by millions of tourists. The information is structured in a clearer way, with beautiful maps and monochromatic illustrations. We designed the format in all its components and then the books were developed inside the publishing house with our supervision.

Stasera

Tg2

RAI, Tg2, Graphics and Set Design, Italy, 1988
This all-encompassing program for the Italian second channel TV included the new logo, all special program logos and the sets' designs. We also introduced the simultaneous presence of words and images in the news broadcast. It was a landmark project based on clear design, devoid of meaningless trends; the impact has been long-lasting. We also designed a special chair for the interviews; made by Poltrona Frau, the chair became extremely popular.

Our B

WTC
OUR BODONI LIGHT

abcdefghijklmnopqrstu
vwxyzæœfiflø

[.,§:;:!?¿¡/'-""* †‡]
1234567890($₠£%)

ABCDEFGHIJKLMNOPQ
RSTUVWXYZ&ÆŒØ

ÁÅÀÇÉÑÔÖÜŻ
áàåçêîñôöüż

WTC
OUR BODONI REGULAR

abcdefghijklmnopqrstu
vwxyzæœfiflø

[.,§:;:!?¿¡/'-""* †‡]
1234567890($₠£%)

ABCDEFGHIJKLMNOPQ
RSTUVWXYZ&ÆŒØ

ÁÅÀÇÉÑÔÖÜŻ
áàåçêîñôöüż

Our Bodoni, Word Typeface Corporation, 1989
We have been asked many times over the years to design typefaces, but always refuse, because we do not feel the need for more. The only necessity, we feel, is to modify some existing typefaces and make them more compatible with contemporary usage. So the first was Bodoni, which we redesigned by increasing the lowercase height, shortening ascenders and descenders and extending the range of weights. We use it all the time and are very comfortable with it. This typeface was co-designed with Tom Carnase.

odoni™

**WTC
OUR BODONI MEDIUM**

abcdefghijklmnopqrstu
vwxyzæœfiflø

[..§::!?¿¡/‵'-"‶* †‡]
1234567890($¢£%)

ABCDEFGHIJKLMNOPQ
RSTUVWXYZ&ÆŒØ

ÁÅÀÇÑÔÕÜŻ
áàåčeîñôŏüż

**WTC
OUR BODONI BOLD**

abcdefghijklmnopqrstu
vwxyzæœfiflø

[..§::!?¿¡/‵'-"‶* †‡]
1234567890($¢£%)

ABCDEFGHIJKLMNOPQ
RSTUVWXYZ&ÆŒØ

ÁÅÀÇÑÔÕÜŻ
áàåčeîñôŏüż

'90

These years are marked by our involvement with clothing design. "If you can't find it, design it." This time we applied our motto to clothing...not fashion, but a timeless garment based on the quality of materials and comfort...easy to pack for travel and easy to wear.

The second most frequent kind of projects were graphic programs for museums and institutions, like the Guggenheim and The American Center in Paris, and the Salone del Mobile in Milano that eventually received the Compasso d'Oro Award.

These are years marked by a secure hand, approaching different projects with determination and enthusiasm, on both sides of the Atlantic.

Here they are, the Vignellis, Lella and Massimo, healthy and happy, wearing clothing from their collection, "Design: Vignelli"....

Design: Vignelli, Clothing Collection, New York, 1991

One day I realized that all my suits were obsolete. I started to look for alternatives, but discovered none. So I decided that I would not be a fashion victim any longer. We have a motto: "If you can't find it, design it." So I went to the office and we started to design and manufacture a line of clothing that follows the body rather than fashion. The task of design is to solve problems; that of fashion is to create them. The basic concept is beautiful materials…light wool, crepe, silk…and easy-to-wear and -pack clothing…beyond fashion, really timeless. We wear them all the time and, for the last fifteen years, we have received nothing but appreciation.

Few Basic Typefaces, Exhibition and Poster, New York 1991

Exasperated by the growing amount of bad typefaces distorted, compressed and extended by people recklessly using the computer, we decided to design an exhibition where we could show work, done by us, using only four typefaces.
The faces were all basic, such as Garamond, Bodoni, Century Expanded and Helvetica.
Displayed on sixteen bins, four for each typeface, one could see a variety of projects, ranging from brochures to books, from packaging to signage, from catalogs to newspapers.
A lecture followed the exhibition and we took a strong position against type proliferation in an attempt to raise world attention to the danger prompted by that irresponsible attitude.
After a worldwide initial reaction to our cry, the frenzy of creating useless typefaces has somehow subsided.
Perhaps that exhibition and our cry were worth it.

In the new computer age the proliferation of typefaces and type manipulations represents a new level of visual pollution threatening our culture. Out of thousands of typefaces, all we need are a few basic ones, and trash the rest. So come and see A Few Basic Typefaces

The Masters Series: Massimo Vignelli
February 22 to March 8, 1991

Reception: Thursday, February 21, 6 to 8 pm
Lecture: Tuesday, February 26, 7 to 9 pm,
School of Visual Arts Amphitheater.

The third in a series of exhibitions honoring the great visual communicators of our time.

Visual Arts Museum, 209 East 23rd Street, NYC, 10010
Museum Hours: Monday to Thursday, 9 am to 8 pm,
Friday, 9 am to 5 pm. Closed Weekends.

The Masters Series is supported in part by a grant from the Architecture, Planning and Design program of the New York State Council on the Arts. ©1991 by the Visual Arts Press, LTD.

Brookstone, Corporate Identity, 1992
Using "Our Bodoni", we designed an identity program for this chain of stores dedicated to no-nonsense products. To express the character of the store, we used plain Kraft paper bags and boxes imprinted and sealed by red tape with the logo in white.

Poltrona Frau, Showrooms and Identity Program, Italy, 1993
In order to achieve instant identification for the Poltrona Frau showrooms, we designed a set of recurrent elements: white walls and curtains, a steel wall, limestone floors and dramatic lighting.

COSMIT, Corporate Identity, Milano, Italy, 1994
COSMIT is the company that organizes and runs all the famous fairs, those dedicated to furniture, lighting, kitchen and bath, etc., in Milan. We have designed for them a comprehensive identification and promotions program, including the signage for the fairgrounds. This program has been in operation for several years and, in 1998, it was awarded the prestigious "Compasso d'Oro" award.

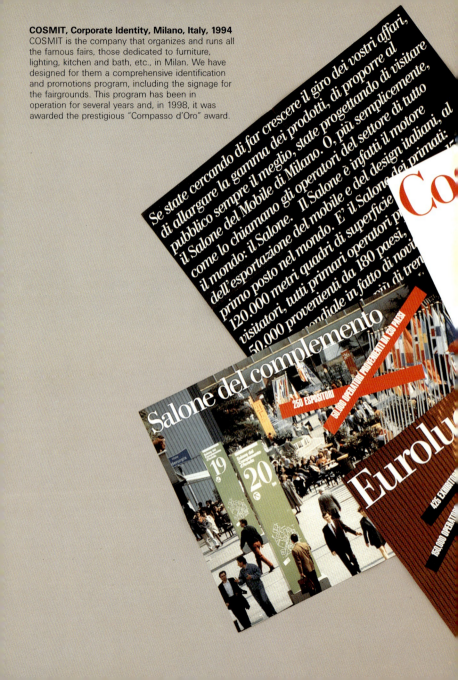

Galleria, Corporate Identity, Madrid, Spain, 1994
This chain of department stores is one of the best in Spain. We devised the tilted "G" as a symbol of action in black and white, a simple, but effective program that is carried through in all the details.

La seduzione. "Sylvia sta per immergersi sotto la cascatella di Fontana di Trevi. Rimane un attimo immobile, i capelli all'indietro, la gonna raccolta sul ventre, le gambe scoperte... La visione di quella donna che passeggia nella vasca tra statue e scrosci d'acqua ha qualcosa di magico. Marcello rimane incantato a guardarla... Un'improvvisa commozione gli stringe la gola... Sylvia si volta con un gesto lieve e ampio delle braccia, come una sacerdotessa che stia per dare inizio ad un misterioso rito pagano..."

Fellini, Exhibition and Catalogue, Italy, 1994
We designed a Fellini exhibition by floating screens with images from his films in a white, almost unreal space. The catalogue has a no-layout layout, consisting of black pages with large text across the spread, and a large picture, full spread. The screen metaphor is clear and direct.

Fassati Wines, Italy, 1994
Since the name of this winery was long, we decided to run it vertically in white against the bottle background. To further promote this wine at the point of sale, we reproduced the bottles and labels on the cartons, to achieve a mass-display effect.

"Barragan", Rizzoli 1992
We had the fortune of meeting the architect
Louis Barragan a few years before his death, and
he showed us some of his buildings. We wanted
to do a book on his work, but unfortunately
after his death his archive was not accessible.
So we requested Armando Salas Portugal,
the photographer of all Barragan's work, the
material for a book on the great architect.
This book is the result, and in it I wrote a
little text on architecture and photography.

"Anyone", IAUS, New York, 1994
This book, part of a series of "ANY" magazine's publication of architectural debates, is printed in red and black on pink paper, and plays with all possibilities offered by positive and negative and color on paper. The sample pages illustrate the notion of scale versus size: scale is intangible and exciting; size is only measurable.

American Center in Paris, Graphic Program, Paris, France, 1994
Again, we played with one-or two-color printing on inexpensive, colored paper to achieve maximum impact at minimum cost. Particular attention was given to the way the mailer unfolded to the final poster size through a succession of well-planned steps.

Steelcase, Showroom and Folder, USA, 1995
This was the second incarnation of a showroom we designed for a special division called "A Design Partnership", a group of several brands under one umbrella. One of the features was a black wall that organized the furniture in use and price categories. With the same graphics, we created a folder of the black wall content...to take the show home with you.

Guggenheim Museum, Graphic Program, New York, 1997

For this prestigious museum, we designed the entire graphic program, from stationery to catalogs, from signage, including signage for the museum's branches overseas, to publications. We preserved the Frank Lloyd Wright typeface for the museum identification and switched to Garamond for text. Of particular interest was the magazine; unfortunately, it had a short life.

Junod, Halo Watch, Switzerland, 1994
The Halo watch has seven rings of anodized aluminum in different colors or frosted plexy. The face is minimally spare.

Junod, Thick and Thin Watch, Switzerland, 1995
The hands, thick for the hours and thin for the minutes, extend beyond the center to add interest to the empty face.

Junod, Dual Time Watch, Switzerland, 2002
Designed for people like me, constantly traveling or living in different time zones and in need of glancing at both times at once.
The red hands for one zone, the black for the other. Simple and easy.

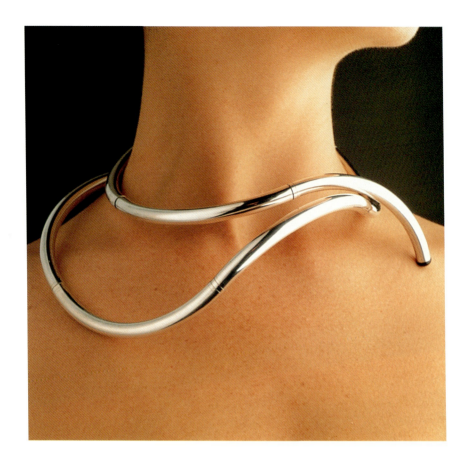

**San Lorenzo, Necklace and Bracelet,
Milano, Italy, 1995**
These silver pieces drastically transform
themselves by pivoting a quarter of a circle
in various ways, each turn more dramatic than
the previous one. The same concept applies
to the necklace and bracelet.
This is one of Lella's sources of
admiration...continuous.

'95

'00

1995 was the year of Benetton, and a provocative project of corporate identity that gave me the opportunity to set up a design office inside the company; actually, a clone of our New York office. A year in which friendship and enthusiasm embraced every facet of this diversified company. These also are the years of large projects worldwide for a variety of mega corporations, like the World Trade Center in Amsterdam, Sea Container in London, Bayerishe Ruck in Munich, Ducati Motors in Italy, JC Decaux in Paris: GNER, the UK Railway, The Italian state railway in Rome and The Museum of Fine Arts in Houston. Years of intense growth, expansion and travel. Maturity brings authority and the projects of these years reflect it. Mass transportation projects require competence, a sense of responsibility and vision.
An array of projects where graphics, interior and product design often were integrated.
More proof that Design is One.

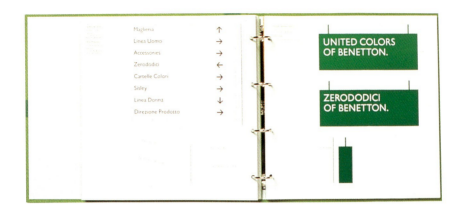

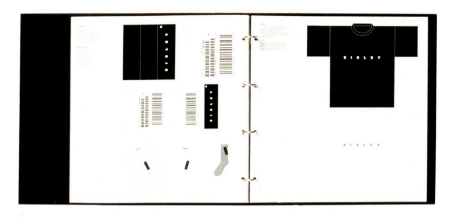

Benetton and Sisley, Corporate Identity, Italy, 1995
We set up a new design office for the company to design and implement a corporate identity covering a wide range of products and applications for both Benetton and Sisley...from logo to labels, packaging to signage...and recorded it in manuals of standards to assure proper implementation through time. A terrific company with a great leader, Luciano Benetton.

World Trade Center, Corporate Identity and Interiors, Amsterdam, 1996
For the World Trade Center at Schipol Airport in Amsterdam, we designed a whimsical logo, graphics and signage plus all public interiors. We commissioned Dale Chihuly, the American glass artist, to design a permanent installation throughout the building. A brilliant concept!

GNER, Corporate Identity and Interiors, London, 1997

Great North Eastern Railway, under new ownership, requested a totally new image change. The logo emphasizes the NE. The train has a new livery, dark blue with a bright red stripe containing all necessary information. It has a crest, a required tradition, and sober interiors for both first and tourist classes. Publications, signage and uniforms for personnel are included in the program and help to carry the identity through every detail.

Ducati, Corporate Identity, Bologna, Italy, 1998
Under new leadership, this glorious brand of motorcycles experienced a rebirth that demanded a new identification program. We purposely refused to embrace the cartoon-popular image and opted for a high-tech, minimalist approach that, after some initial resistance, was embraced by a new set of customers who responded to the new style: a bright red chromotype and Univers italic type. Dramatic new photos produced new connotations, linking the products to their audience.

Seaco, Sea Containers, Corporate Identity, London, 1992–1998
Sea Containers' image was, in great part, carried by its containers, a blue box with the Seaco logo in white with a heavy red band on top of it. I rarely traveled to any city around the world without seeing one of the containers. An effective and ubiquitous brand.

Sea Cat, Ferry Boats, Signage, London, 1998
A new livery was designed for all ferry boats linking the United Kingdom to the continent: a basically white boat with a large logo on its side, making it highly visible.

next pages:
Guggenheim Museum, Signage, Bilbao, Spain, 1998
Few buildings in the world have received as much attention as this Frank Gehry masterpiece. We were lucky to be the designers of the signage and auditorium seating. Most of the signage is on movable pedestals to respond to the museum's flexibility needs.

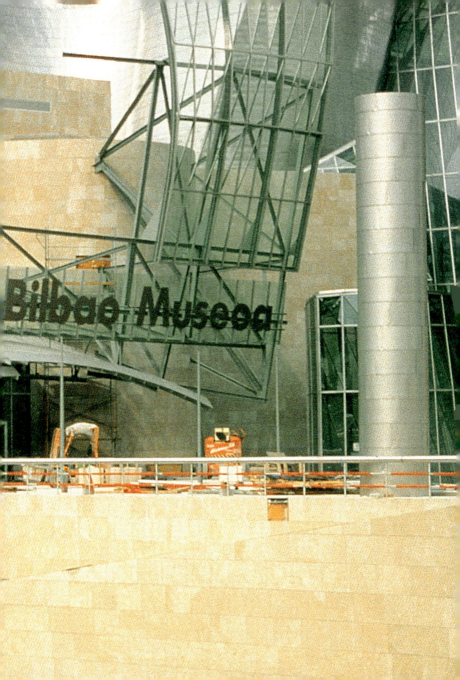

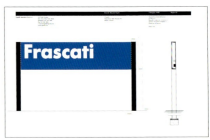

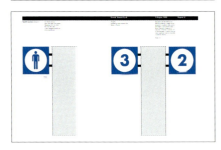

Ferrovie dello Stato, Station Signs, Italy, 1999
We were given the assignment of designing the sign system for the major and minor stations of the Italian Railway. The program still is in its implementation phase, but wherever it has been applied, it makes a substantial difference in the efficiency and look of the stations. In this spread are signs for the minor stations. In the next spread are some of the signs at Termini Station in Rome.

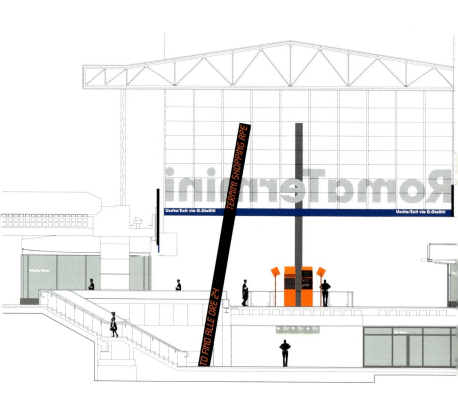

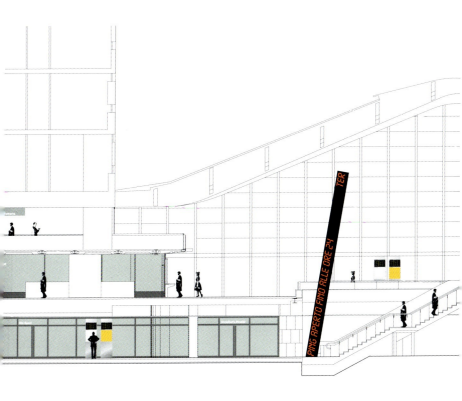

JC Decaux, Street Furniture, Paris, 1999
For this leading company of street furniture and outdoor advertising, we designed a whole line of street furniture, including newsstands, bus shelters and public toilets. We still have the hope of seeing some of them somewhere one day soon.

Museum of Fine Arts, Houston, Graphic Program and Signage, Houston, 1999
This program encompassed every printed piece, from logo to stationery, invitations to publications, and all signage, from building identification to Donors' Wall, garage to restaurant. The building sign, of monumental scale, is a special design requested by the architect. The Donors' Wall dominates the atrium with its monumental scale. A comprehensive program beautifully implemented by the museum's staff.

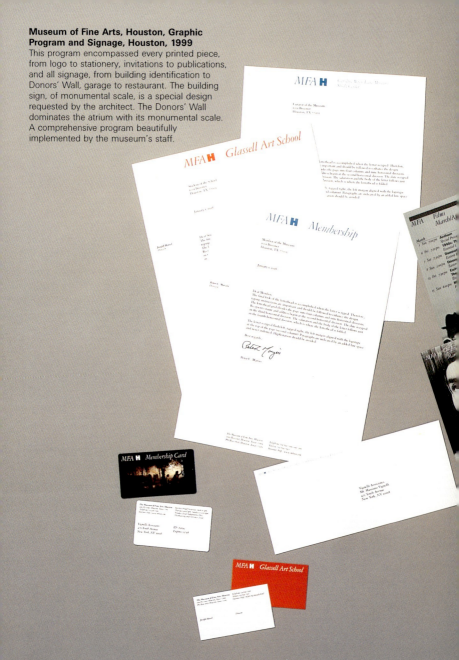

MUSEUM OF FINE ARTS, HOUSTO

HOUSTON ENDOWMENT INC. CAROLINE WIESS LAW THE B
HARRY S. AND ISABEL C. CAMERON FOUNDATION FRANCI AN
LEE AND JOE JAMAIL THE KRESGE FOUNDATION MR. AND MR.
ISLA AND THOMAS R. RECKLING III FAYEZ SAROFIM/FAYEZ SARO
ISABEL B. AND WALLACE S. WILSON THE WORTHAM FOUN
LAURA LEE AND JACK BLANTON BMC SOFTWARE CITY O
THE ELEANOR AND FRANK FREED FOUNDATION THE FRIEDKIN
NATIONAL ENDOWMENT FOR THE HUMANITIES TASSIE AND
A I M MANAGEMENT GROUP INC. MR. AND MRS. LOUIS K. ADLER
ANDERSEN CONSULTING M.D. ANDERSON FOUNDATION A
BAKER & BOTTS, LLP MR. AND MRS. A.L. BALLARD BANK OF A
CAROLYN AND JOHN BOOKOUT THE BRENER AND HELLMUN
BURLINGTON RESOURCES CHARLES BUTT CHARLENE AND PHIL
COOPER INDUSTRIES ROSANETTE AND HARRY CULLEN MR.
ALISON AND ROBERT DUNCAN BRENDA AND JOHN H. DUNCAN
TILMAN AND PAIGE FERTITTA JERRY AND NANETTE FINGER FOUND
FOLEY'S LISA FORD MR. AND MRS. RUSSELL M. FRANKEL FULBRI
THE JAMES W. GLANVILLE FAMILY FOUNDATION MRS. JAMES W
JEAN CURRY GLASSELL GWENDOLYN HOLMES GOFFE GOLDM
WILLIAM RANDOLPH HEARST FOUNDATION ALBERT AND ETHEL
THE HOBBY FAMILY MARJORIE G. AND EVAN C. HORNING
THE RANDALL HAGE JAMAIL FAMILY THE ROBERT LEE JAMAIL FAM
THE MAVIS P. KELSEY, SR. FAMILY KATHRYN AND JAMES KETE
A. RONALD AND JANE H. LERNER LIATIS FOUNDATION IN MEMOR
FRANCES AND PETER MARZIO CARROLL AND HARRIS MASTERSON
THE MOSBACHER FAMILY IN MEMORY OF JANE MOSBACHE
NANCY NELSON BROWN NELLEY WILLIAM WALTER NEGL
FRED AND MABEL R. PARKS FOUNDATION PARNASSUS FO
MR. AND MRS. EDWARD RANDALL ELIZA LOVETT RANDALL FAIRFA
H. JOHN AND DIANE M. RIL NANCY AND CLIVE RUNNE
JOAN WEINGARTEN SCHNITZE R. AND MRS. H. IRVING SCHWE
CAROL CLARK TATKON TENN THE TEXACO FOUNDATION
UNION TEXAS PETROLEUM ISON & ELKINS LLP WILLIA
LYNN AND OSCAR WYATT M D MRS. MICHAEL S. ZILKHA

'03

The end of the year 2000 was also the end of our office lease. An enormous rent increase forced us to leave our beloved place, and gave us the opportunity to rescale our activities.

The advent of the computer makes possible work with a minimal staff and increased mobility. Our work now concentrates on prestigious and imaginative clients, mostly in Europe, involving, once again, the whole field of design, from graphics to packaging, from exhibitions to interiors. Again, several beautiful books of architecture and art required considerable time.

This is a time to rethink our priorities, perhaps to re-order the ambitious workload and travel schedules we have known for some 50 years. This is an extremely difficult goal to achieve when passion, enthusiasm and curiosity still possess our souls.

Poltrona Frau, Showrooms, Italy, 2000
Starting a new program with the Milano showroom, Lella designed a series of showrooms throughout Italy, some in new locations, some in historic buildings. A new vocabulary of elements has been established, such as recessed lighting strips in the ceilings, the use of frosted mirror walls, limestone floors, and open spaces to highlight the products. An overall rarified atmosphere conveys a sense of elegance and modernity to the products. The examples shown are from different showrooms throughout Italy.

Murano, Glass from the Olnick Spanu Collection, Exhibition and Catalog, USA, Italy, 2001

To display this precious and rare collection of Murano glass, designed mostly by Carlo Scarpa and other top designers, we created a traveling exhibition that is basically a lightbox to highlight glass colors and forms. A catalogue with beautiful, sensitive photographs by our son, Luca Vignelli, fulfills the family engagement on this project, and reveals our love for Murano glass.

Feudi di San Gregorio, Packaging and Graphic Program, Italy, 2001
Retaining the mosaic picture from the previous labels, we redesigned them by adding another square under the mosaic for the wine name on a black background. We concentrated all legal text on the back panel and left only two small squares in the front. A minimal, but strong approach: the design received the Italian "Oscar" award for wine labels in 2003.

next page:
Feudi di San Gregorio Stand at the VinItaly Fair in Verona, Italy, 2001
A two-story structure that could be assembled in various configurations, according to needs. The structure, in galvanized steel, gives the stand a permanent. rather then ephemeral, look.

**Ognissole Winery,
Packaging Program
Italy, 2002**
Another example of
minimal labeling.

Vigne di Mezzo Winery, Packaging Program, Italy, 2003
Again, a label for a great wine from the south of Italy, with an ancient greek coin reproduction, to link the wine with his history and territory.

"Pete Turner African Journey", New York, 2002
A book of great African images by a master of monochrome photography. An ancient continent seen with modern eyes by a sophisticated artist.

"KPF", Rizzoli International, New York, 2003
A portfolio of the worldwide activity by the prolific architectural office of Kohn Pedersen Fox Associates. The layouts relate to and continue a format established in volume one.

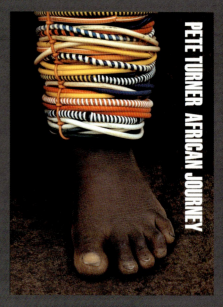

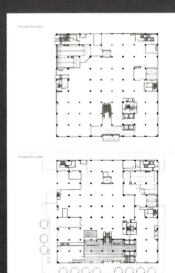

**"Tadao Ando, Light and Water",
Monacelli Press, 2003**
The play of light and water in the buildings of the great architect Tadao Ando. The work of a great poet. A book I designed with great love for one of my favorite architects.

**"Michele Oka Doner", New York,
Hutson Hills Press, 2003**
A book on the work of an artist who can transform nature into works of art of hovering beauty. The very simple and focused layouts are a sign of respect for this beautiful work.

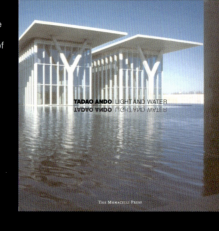

**"Dumbarton Oaks", Monacelli Press,
New York, 2002**
The story of this romantic Washington garden with sensitive images through the year's seasons. This is a book in two parts: history of the garden and a photographic portfolio, and the layouts follow this format.

"Harry Seidler's Grand Tour", Taschen, 2003
The great monuments of the world seen by the eyes of a great architect on a lifetime quest for the best. A guidebook designed with passion and measure. A labor of love.

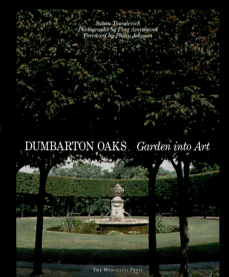

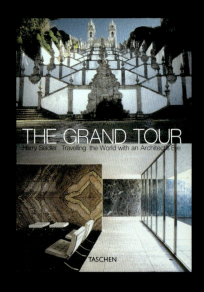

Above:
Wild violets owned with crab-apple petals.

Opposite:
View south through the Plum Walk, installed in 1936.

Following pages:
The hillside along Midsummer's Allée.

6 Rome, Colosseum, 70-82 AD
The most magnificent of many Roman amphitheatres, accommodated 60,000 spectators in an amazing engineering feat for its time.

7 Taormina Theatre
The originally Greek and later Roman Theatre overlooks the beautiful coast of Sicily.

8-10 Rome, The Pantheon, 118-126 AD
The circular building has the same diameter and height of about 50 m - an engineering triumph built in successively diminishing rings of stone with an open oculus in the centre.

11 Rome, The Pantheon, 118-126 AD
Exterior of the portico.

The Italian Avant Garde in Car Design, Exhibition, New York, 2002
Fabulous Italian cars of all times silhouetted by walls of light and images in the bare space of a huge Armory. The cars were parked on the sides of a virtual road delineated by rows of parallel walls of light.

Massimo Vignelli

Massimo Vignelli, born in Milan, studied architecture in Milan and Venice. Massimo and Lella Vignelli established the Vignelli Office of Design and Architecture in Milan in 1960.
In 1965, Massimo Vignelli became co-founder and design director of Unimark International Corporation, before opening the offices of Vignelli Associates in 1971 and Vignelli Designs in 1978. Massimo Vignelli is the co-founder and President of Vignelli Associates and Chief Executive Officer of Vignelli Designs in New York.
His work includes graphic and corporate identity programs, publication designs, architectural graphics, and exhibition, interior, furniture, and consumer product designs for many leading American and European companies and institutions.

Mr. Vignelli's work has been published and exhibited throughout the world and entered in the permanent collections of several museums; notably, the Museum of Modern Art, the Metropolitan Museum of Art, the Brooklyn Museum and the Cooper-Hewitt Museum in New York; the Musée des Arts Décoratifs in Montreal; and the Die Neue Sammlung in Munich.
Mr. Vignelli has taught and lectured on design in the major cities and universities in the United States and abroad. For the past ten years he has taught a summer course at the Harvard University Graduate School of Design. He is a past president of the Alliance Graphique Internationale (AGI) and the American Institute of Graphic Arts (AIGA) and a vice president of The Architectural League.
A feature-length television program on the Vignellis' work has been aired worldwide. Exhibitions of Vignelli Associates were held in Boston, New York, St. Louis, Los Angeles and in 1982 in Milano, Italy. A major exhibition of the Vignelli's work toured Europe between 1989 and 1993, and was featured in St. Petersburg, Moscow, Helsinki, London, Budapest, Barcelona, Copenhagen, Munich, Prague and Paris.

Among Massimo Vignelli's many awards: Gran Premio Triennale di Milano, 1964; Compasso d'Oro, awarded by the Italian Association for Industrial Design (ADI), 1964 and 1998; the 1973 Industrial Arts Medal of the American Institute of Architects (AIA); the 1982 Art Directors Club Hall of Fame; the 1983 AIGA Gold Medal; the first Presidential Design Award, presented by President Ronald Reagan in 1985, for the National Park Service Publications Program; the 1988 Interior Design Hall of Fame; the 1991 National Arts Club Gold Medal for Design; the 1992 Interior Product Designers Fellowship of Excellence; the 1995 Brooklyn Museum Design Award for Lifetime Achievement; and the 2001 Russel Wright Award for Design Excellence.
He has been awarded an Honorary Doctorate in Architecture from the University of Venice, Italy and Honorary Doctorates in Fine Arts from Parsons School of Design, New York, Pratt Institute, Brooklyn, Rhode Island School of Design, Providence, the Corcoran School of Art, Washington, D.C., and the Art Center College of Design, Pasadena, California, the Rochester Institute of Technology, Rochester, New York.
In 1996 he received the Honorary Royal Designer for Industry Award from the Royal Society of Arts, London.
In 2003 Lella and Massimo Vignelli received the National Design Lifetime Achievement Award.

A comprehensive monograph *Design:Vignelli* was published by Rizzoli International.

Lella Vignelli

Lella Valle Vignelli is the co-founder and Chief Executive Officer of Vignelli Associates and President of Vignelli Designs. Her work is widely featured in design publications in the United States and abroad. Examples of her designs are in the permanent collections of numerous museums, including the Museum of Modern Art, the Cooper-Hewitt Museum and the Metropolitan Museum of Art in New York; the Musée des Arts Décoratifs in Montreal; and Die Neue Sammlung in Munich. Lella and Massimo Vignellis' work has been the subject of a feature-length television program broadcast worldwide. A major exhibition of their designs toured Europe between 1989 and 1993, and was featured in St. Petersburg, Moscow, Helsinki, London, Budapest, Barcelona, Copenhagen, Munich, Prague and Paris. Other exhibitions were held in Boston, New York, St. Louis, Los Angeles and Milan.

Lella Vignelli is a frequent speaker and juror for national and international design organizations. She has been the recipient of many awards including Honorary Doctorates from the Parsons School of Design, New York and the Corcoran School of Art, Washington, D.C.; the American Institute of Architects (AIA) Industrial Arts Medal, 1973; AIGA Gold Medal, 1983; Interior Design Hall of Fame, 1988; National Arts Club Gold Medal for Design, 1991; Interior Product Designers Fellowship of Excellence, 1992; the Brooklyn Museum Design Award for Lifetime Achievement, 1995; the Russel Wright Award of Design Excellence 2001; and the President Medal of the Rochester Institute of Technology, 2002.

Lella Vignelli received the "Dottore Architetto" degree from the University of Venice, and became a registered architect in Milan in 1962. In 1958, she received a fellowship at the School of Architecture, Massachusetts Institute of Technology, Cambridge. Prior to establishing the Vignelli office of Design and Architecture in Milan (1961) she worked with Skidmore, Owings & Merrill, Chicago. In 1965 she headed the interiors department for Unimark International in Milan and moved with them to New York in 1966. With Massimo she founded the firm of Vignelli Associates in 1971 in New York and Vignelli Designs in 1978.

Every effort has been made to trace the original
source of copyright material contained in this book.
The publishers would be pleased to hear from
copyright holders to rectify any errors or omissions.
The information and illustrations in this publication
have been prepared and supplied by Massimo
Vignelli. While all reasonable efforts have been made
to ensure accuracy, the publishers do not, under any
circumstances, accept responsibility for errors,
omissions and representations expressed or implied.